# Table of Contents

Executive Summary ............................................................................................................. 3

Chapter 1. Introduction ...................................................................................................... 5

Chapter 2: What is the Rationale for Offering a Financing Program? ............................... 8

Chapter 3: Is Financing the Best (or only) Option? ......................................................... 16

Chapter 4: What Financing Program Features Best Drive Demand? .............................. 19

Chapter 5. Evaluating Key Questions .............................................................................. 22

Chapter 6. Conclusions .................................................................................................... 29

References ........................................................................................................................ 30

Appendix A. Experimental Design Methods & Practical Implementation Guidance ..... 32

## Acknowledgements

The work described in this report was funded by the Department of Energy Office of Energy Efficiency and Renewable Energy, Strategic Programs under Contract No. DE-AC02-05CH11231. We appreciate the support and guidance of Seungwook Ma, Christopher Lohmann, Johanna Zetterberg, and Carla Frisch at DOE EERE. We would like to thank the following individuals for providing thoughtful comments and input on a review draft of this report: Elena Alschuler (DOE), Casey Bell (ACEEE), Colin Bishopp (DOE), Craig Diamond (CEFC), Steve Dunn (DOE), George Edgar (WECC), Sandy Fazelli (NASEO), Jennifer Finnigan (SnoPUD), Bryan Garcia (CEFIA), Ken Gilligan (Yale), Matt Golden (Efficiency.org), Paula Grigolii Pedro (UC Berkeley), Philip Henderson (NRDC), Jess Kincaid (OR DOE), Chris Kramer (EFG), Peter Miller (NRDC), Joanne Morin (CEE), Steve Nadel (ACEEE), Steve Schiller (LBNL), Karen Palmer (RFF), Richard Sedano (RAP) and Peter Thompson (LBNL). While we benefitted immensely from the wisdom of the many people who gave feedback on this report, all mistakes are our own.

## Disclaimer

This document was prepared as an account of work sponsored by the United States Government. While this document is believed to contain correct information, neither the United States Government nor any agency thereof, nor The Regents of the University of California, nor any of their employees, makes any warranty, express or implied, or assumes any legal responsibility for the accuracy, completeness, or usefulness of any information, apparatus, product, or process disclosed, or represents that its use would not infringe privately owned rights. Reference herein to any specific commercial product, process, or service by its trade name, trademark, manufacturer, or otherwise, does not necessarily constitute or simply its endorsement, recommendation, or favoring by the United States Government or any agency thereof, or The Regents of the University of California. The views and opinions of authors expressed herein do not necessarily state or reflect those of the United States Government or any agency thereof or The Regents of the University of California. Ernest Orlando Lawrence Berkeley National Laboratory is an equal opportunity employer.

# Getting the Biggest Bang for the Buck
*Exploring the Rationales and Design Options for Energy Efficiency Financing Programs*

## Executive Summary

Many state policymakers and utility regulators have established aggressive energy efficiency (EE) savings targets which will necessitate investing billions of dollars in existing buildings – and tax payer and utility bill payer funding is a small fraction of the total investment needed.[1] Given this challenge, some EE program administrators are exploring ways to increase their reliance on financing with the aim of amplifying the impact of limited program monies.[2] While financing is potentially an attractive tool for increasing program leverage and mitigating the rate impacts of utility customer-funded efficiency programs, administrators can face difficult choices between allocating funds to financing or to other approaches designed to overcome a broader set of barriers to consumer investment in EE. Robust assessments of financing's role in reducing energy use in buildings are necessary to help policymakers and program administrators make better choices about how to allocate limited resources to achieve cost-effective energy savings at scale.

In order to better understand what EE financing can be reasonably expected to achieve, and for whom, this report is organized around three levels of inquiry (Figure 1), from the most fundamental (level 1) to the most detailed (level 3).

**Figure 1:** Three levels of inquiry to inform the design of energy efficiency financing programs.

1. **What is the rationale for offering energy efficiency financing?**
(i.e. What problem(s) are you solving?)

2. **Does financing address key barriers better or at a lower cost than other options for intervention?**
(i.e. Is financing the best option for solving this problem?)

3. **What specific financing program design features best drive demand for energy efficiency?**
(i.e. How do you design the financing program for greatest impact?)

---

[1] For example, in California, it is estimated that $70 billion of EE investment in existing buildings will be required over the next decade to achieve the state's policy goals – only a fraction of which will be provided by ratepayer funding (HB&C 2011).
[2] A few examples of this increasing reliance on financing: In California, the Public Utilities Commission has approved $200 million of pilot programs to test whether transitional ratepayer support can trigger self-supporting programs (CPUC 2013). In Connecticut, the Clean Energy Finance & Investment Authority's 2013-2015 Strategic Plan notes that its programs "will reflect the strategic transition away from technology innovation, workforce development, formal education and subsidies towards a focus on low-cost financing of clean energy deployment…(in order to) seek to leverage ratepayer dollars…"(CEFIA 2013). In New York, the $1 billion Green Bank's goals include overcoming disparate one-time subsidies and offering public credit and investment programs that require only a small amount of government funds (Cuomo 2013).

For each of these three levels of inquiry, the report describes key uncertainties that must be resolved in order to better understand the role of financing in delivering cost-effective energy savings. Examples include:

- What market segments or types of efficiency improvements are currently underserved by financial markets and why?
- Is financing an effective tool for driving consumer EE adoption? For which consumers and at what cost? What other strategies should be combined with financing to maximally increase EE adoption at the lowest possible cost?
- Does financing for EE have lower participant defaults and delinquencies than financing for other property improvements? If so, is the default rate low enough to warrant substantial improvements to the interest rates, loan lengths and/or underwriting for private financial products? What impact do these improved features have on consumer EE adoption?
- Does sufficient consumer demand exist today to warrant program investments in aggregation and securitization infrastructure, or should interventions simply focus on increasing the volume of standardized financial products?
- Are novel financing products more effective in overcoming barriers to EE adoption than traditional financing products?
- Are consumers as (or more) likely to adopt targeted EE improvements if offered financing or rebates (or other support such as technical assistance)? Do completed EE projects deliver greater energy savings if program financing is used (or available) compared to rebates (or other strategies)?

This report offers a starting place for developing a better understanding of financing's role in driving cost-effective EE adoption. We encourage program administrators and policymakers to identify those issues and questions that are most relevant to their program's success and to begin to test whether their assumptions are correct. Not every program needs to answer every question – as more and more programs actively explore these questions, lessons learned can be shared.

# Chapter 1. Introduction

Many state policymakers and utility regulators have established aggressive energy efficiency (EE) savings targets which will necessitate investing billions of dollars in existing buildings – and tax payer and utility bill payer funding is a small fraction of the total investment needed.[3] Given this challenge, some EE program administrators are exploring ways to increase their reliance on financing with the aim of amplifying the impact of limited program monies.[4] While financing is potentially an attractive tool for increasing program leverage and mitigating the rate impacts of utility customer-funded EE programs, it is critical that policymakers and program administrators gain a better understanding of what financing can be reasonably expected to achieve, and for whom – and how to design financing programs to both maximize short-term impacts and to learn from experience over time.

## Background

Financing has historically been a small part of the portfolio of energy efficiency program offerings. Because these initiatives have been small and often secondary to rebate and other programs, the efficacy of financing programs in delivering cost-effective energy savings has typically been assessed qualitatively (Cadmus 2012), or not at all (beyond simply tracking the financing amounts issued). In most cases, these initiatives have failed to achieve significant market penetration (Fuller 2009, Hayes et al. 2011). In a world of limited program budgets, administrators can face difficult choices between allocating funds to financing or to other approaches designed to overcome a broader set of barriers to consumer investment in EE.

As some policymakers and program administrators consider shifting the traditional mix of program offerings to rely more heavily on financing, it is important to undertake a more rigorous assessment of the ability of financing to overcome barriers to consumer adoption of property improvements that deliver cost-effective incremental energy savings – and be able to compare the impacts of investments in financing programs (e.g., cost and level of energy savings, rate impacts) to other programmatic strategies. Robust assessments of financing's role in reducing energy use in buildings will help policymakers and program administrators make better choices about how to allocate limited tax payer and utility bill payer resources.

## Report Objectives

The primary objectives of this report are to articulate the rationales for offering financing programs, to highlight key policy and program design questions regarding the role of financing for which we need better answers, and to offer guidance to administrators on how financing programs can be designed and evaluated to assess their efficacy. Some of these questions can be tested directly by assessing the impacts of specific program designs; other questions will require more qualitative market research, and

---

[3] For example, in California, it is estimated that $70 billion of EE investment in existing buildings will be required over the next decade to achieve the state's policy goals – only a fraction of which will be provided by ratepayer funding (HB&C 2011).
[4] A few examples of this increasing reliance on financing: In California, the Public Utilities Commission has approved $200 million of pilot programs to test whether transitional ratepayer support can trigger self-supporting programs (CPUC 2013). In Connecticut, the Clean Energy Finance & Investment Authority's 2013-2015 Strategic Plan notes that its' programs "will reflect the strategic transition away from technology innovation, workforce development, formal education and subsidies towards a focus on low-cost financing of clean energy deployment…(in order to) seek to leverage ratepayer dollars…"(CEFIA 2013). In New York, the $1 billion Green Bank's goals include overcoming disparate one-time subsidies and offering public credit and investment programs that require only a small amount of government funds (Cuomo 2013).

observation over time. We divide these questions into three "levels" of inquiry, represented in Figure 2, from the most fundamental (level 1) to the most detailed (level 3).

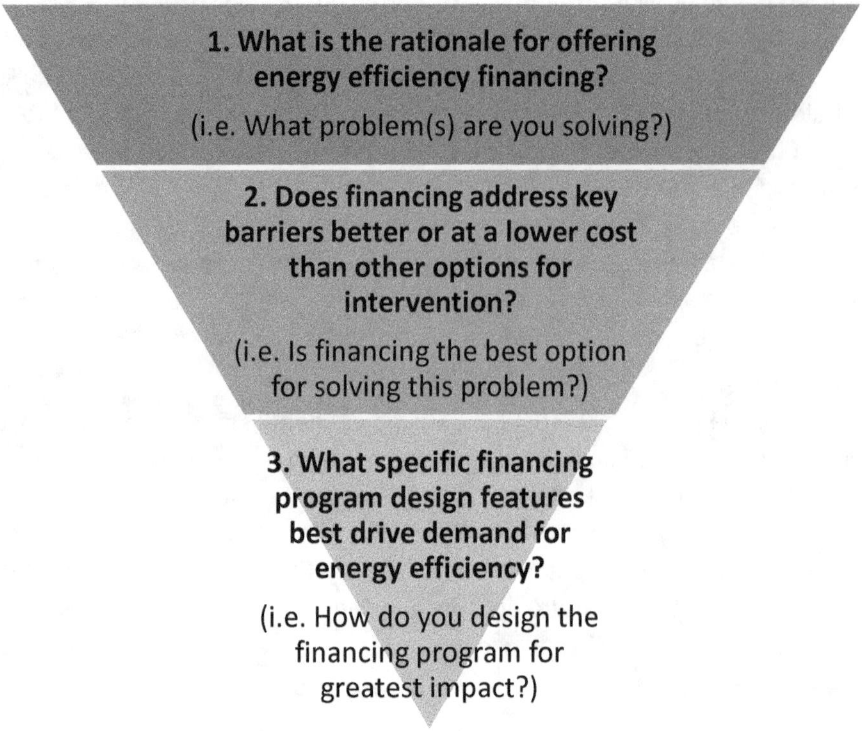

**1. What is the rationale for offering energy efficiency financing?**
(i.e. What problem(s) are you solving?)

**2. Does financing address key barriers better or at a lower cost than other options for intervention?**
(i.e. Is financing the best option for solving this problem?)

**3. What specific financing program design features best drive demand for energy efficiency?**
(i.e. How do you design the financing program for greatest impact?)

**Figure 2:** Levels of inquiry to inform the design of energy efficiency financing programs.

## Report Organization

Level 1, described in the next chapter, explores several possible rationales for devoting tax payer or utility bill payer funds to efficiency financing programs; understanding the "problem" that financing is intended to address is vital to tracking and evaluating the ability of a program to effectively address barrier(s) to increased EE adoption. Level 2, discussed in Chapter 3, explores the efficacy of financing *relative* to the many other options for market intervention. Level 3, described in Chapter 4, explores key questions that must be resolved in designing effective financing programs once a program administrator determines that support for financing is needed.

In Chapter 5, we briefly describe several methods that can be utilized to address these questions: (a) qualitative market research that could include market assessments and participant surveys, (b) the analysis of standardized financing program data, ideally compared across multiple jurisdictions, and (c) the use of experiments to more definitively assess program impacts and the efficacy of program design features. In Appendix A, we offer a more detailed description of experimental design techniques and examples of how these techniques can be used to answer key financing questions.

## How to Read This Report

This report provides an overview of the broad motivations for offering financing initiatives that facilitate efficiency investments across consumer segments as well as key questions that must be resolved to assess the efficacy of these strategies. Rather than attempt an exhaustive catalog of the range of uncertainties about the impacts of these programs on delivering incremental energy savings, we offer illustrative examples of those questions that we believe are most important to answer based on our experience working with EE financing program administrators, policymakers, financial institutions and EE service providers. It is essential to ask the key questions identified in this report with an appreciation that both their importance and their answers may differ substantially between, and within, consumer classes depending upon local market conditions, targeted improvements and policymakers and program administrator goals. We encourage stakeholders to identify the issues and uncertainties most relevant for their target markets and design future programs to include thought out plans for answering key program impact and design issues.

## Chapter 2: What is the Rationale for Offering a Financing Program?

At the most fundamental level, the rationale(s) for offering financing programs must be clearly established so that program administrators have an understanding of the problem(s) they are aiming to solve, and can recognize "success" when (and if) it occurs. Many state policymakers and utility regulators acknowledge that EE has substantial public and energy system benefits. However, consumers often invest in EE at lower levels than is socially-optimal given the combination of public, energy system, and private benefits (Golove & Eto 1996, Jaffe & Stavins 1994). A variety of barriers to broader consumer EE adoption have been cited in the literature, including the fact that EE often has "high first costs" (IEA 2008; Jaffe & Stavins 1994). While these up-front costs are often recouped over the lifetime of the efficiency measures through energy savings, some consumers lack the financial means or the willingness to use their limited existing resources to make the initial purchase of high-efficiency measures.

These high first costs have been one impetus for utilities, states, and local governments to experiment with financing programs, where consumers are offered some form of program-supported financing to help pay for efficiency improvements.[5]

**1. What is the rationale for offering energy efficiency financing?**
(i.e. What problem(s) are you solving?)

Several cases may be made that today's EE financing market warrants tax payer or utility bill payer intervention due to either (a) market failure or (b) the broader set of goals (e.g., energy savings, emission reductions) of tax payer and bill payer funds relative to private monies, which are typically deployed purely to seek financial return. The problems that tax payer or bill payer-funded financing programs are seeking to solve need to be clearly identified and tested to ensure that (a) the problem(s) exists and (b) allocating funds to programmatic financing initiatives effectively addresses the problem(s).

Depending on a program's objectives and the willingness of private markets (e.g., lenders, investors) to respond to program initiatives, these interventions may be temporary or long-term. The motivations for these programmatic interventions are potentially numerous, but based on our experience reviewing financing programs, we discuss five common program rationales below:

  A. New financial products are needed to overcome barriers specific to energy efficiency;
  B. Some consumer market segments are under-served by private markets;

---

[5] We describe "offering financing programs" in the broadest sense – this may take the form of direct provision of public or ratepayer capital, direct or indirect support for private sector financial products (e.g., credit enhancement, co-marketing, customer intake), enabling or offering of novel financial products (e.g. on-bill financing) or some combination of these.

C. More information is needed before private markets can provide appropriate financial products;
D. Financial product standardization and aggregation are needed for the private markets to deliver attractive capital, and;
E. Larger consumer cost contributions are needed to increase the leverage of limited tax payer or utility bill payer funding.

Historically, Rationales A and B were typically the primary motivators for policymakers and program administrators to support EE financing initiatives as they sought to overcome barriers faced by individual consumers. Through time, these rationales have expanded to include broader "market failures" like those highlighted in Rationales C and D. More recently, the attention being paid to financing has focused on the need to increase consumer cost contributions to EE projects in order to achieve significant EE savings goals in the context of limited program budgets (Rationale E).

In the following sections, we describe each rationale and raise questions that program administrators should consider in program design and evaluation in order to determine whether program results support the rationale for operating them; and what, if any, program modifications are needed for the programs to effectively deliver on program administrator goals.

## Rationale A: New financial products are needed to overcome efficiency's specific barriers

The high up-front cost of some energy efficiency measures is one of several barriers to broader consumer adoption of these improvements. Some new financial products have special features with the potential to address both the high first cost barrier and other barriers such as renter/owner split incentives, long project paybacks, and balance sheet treatment that lead to consumer under-investment in EE in certain market segments.[6] For example, two novel financial products that have garnered significant attention are Property Assessed Clean Energy (PACE) and On-Bill Financing (OBF).[7,8] PACE involves financing energy improvements through a special property tax assessment, which is typically senior to all other debt on a property, including the first mortgage.[9] OBF involves repaying financing for energy improvements on the customer's utility bill, often secured by the possibility of service disconnection for non-payment.[10] These products' novel security may offer value to lenders and investors that can be leveraged to expand consumer access to attractive capital beyond that which private markets can deliver through traditional financial products.[11] In Table 1, we highlight other potential advantages of these novel

---

[6] Balance sheet treatment refers to whether financing is treated as an "on-balance sheet" or "off-balance sheet" obligation for accounting purposes. "Off-balance sheet" treatment enables non-residential customers to finance EE improvements without increasing their debt-to-equity ratio, a metric which is studied closely by investors and often capped by lenders. For more information on the advantages and disadvantages of off-balance sheet financing, consult an accounting professional.

[7] Other novel financing products may include traditional financing products whose underwriting takes specific account of a property or project's energy efficient features (e.g., Energy Efficient Mortgages, HUD Powersaver Loans, HUD Green Refinance Plus Multifamily Mortgages).

[8] Some stakeholders use the term On-Bill Financing to describe on-bill programs that are capitalized with tax payer or utility bill payer capital while using the term On-Bill Repayment to characterize on-bill programs capitalized with private capital. For the purposes of this report, we use the term On-Bill Financing in reference to all on-bill programs, regardless of capital source.

[9] More information on PACE available here: http://www1.eere.energy.gov/wip/solutioncenter/pace.html

[10] More information on OBF available here: http://www1.eere.energy.gov/wip/solutioncenter/onbillrepayment.html

[11] While novel security may expand customer access to capital, it is important to proceed carefully to ensure that customers are able and willing to repay these novel products as the consequences of non-payment are severe (e.g., foreclosure, utility service disconnection) and high default levels may not be tolerable to policymakers.

financial products (in addition to their potential to broaden consumer access to capital)—and uncertainty about their value—relative to commonly-used traditional financial products.

**Table 1:** Comparison of PACE and OBF programs with standard existing financing products.

| Financial Product | Security[12] | Overcomes Renter/Owner Split Incentives? | Overcomes Long Project Paybacks That May Exceed Tenancy/Ownership? | Overcomes Balance Sheet Barriers? |
|---|---|---|---|---|
| **Unsecured Loan** | None | No | No | No |
| **Mortgage** | Lien on consumer's property | No | No | No |
| **PACE** | Super-senior lien on consumer's property | Maybe.* If lease contracts include the pass through of property taxes to tenants | Maybe.** PACE assessments are transferable from one property owner to the next. | Maybe. Uncertainty remains about whether PACE can be treated as an "off-balance sheet" obligation. |
| **OBF** | Tariff on property's (or unit's) utility meter | Maybe.* If tenants pay utility bills. | Maybe.** In some cases, OBF tariffs automatically or, with occupant consent may, transfer from one tenant or owner to the next. | Maybe. Uncertainty about whether OBF can be treated as an "off-balance sheet" obligation. |

*The value of PACE and OBF for overcoming the "split incentives" barrier remains uncertain and is based on the assumption that tenants will value the installed improvements and be willing to pay for them through a charge on their utility bill or an increase in their rent.

**The value of "transferability" for overcoming the "long project payback" barrier remains uncertain and is based on the assumption that subsequent tenants/owners will value the improvements for which they are being asked to assume the obligation to make debt payments.

Broadly-available energy performance guarantees and energy savings insurance products are also promising tools that can reduce the risk that a consumer will not realize the energy savings they are expecting. While guarantees and insurance products are not financial products themselves, they may help to catalyze the delivery of innovative financial products whose security is tied to these energy savings and energy service delivery models. For example, these products might enable third parties to finance the energy improvements and consumers to simply pay for energy savings as they are realized rather than taking on financing (and project performance risk) themselves.[13] Given their promise, there may be a policy justification for offering tax payer or utility bill payer funds to support the development and implementation of these energy savings performance risk reduction products in some markets.

---

[12] Financial product security refers to what "secures" a loan or lease in the event that a customer defaults. For example, home mortgages are secured by the financial institution's right to foreclose on one's home should a customer default on their loan repayment obligation.

[13] These guarantees typically involve complex, long-term contractual arrangements related to ensuring that "baseline" energy use conditions persist in facilities throughout the life of the guarantee. In commercial buildings, consumers may be reluctant to utilize these contracts due to the loss of long-term flexibility they may face in altering building occupancy, production processes or other factors that may drive their core profitability.

Key questions:
- Are novel financing products more effective in overcoming barriers to energy efficiency adoption than traditional financing products?
- Do specific features such as novel security, threat of utilities disconnection, alternative underwriting, or others lead to lower consumer defaults and delinquencies or higher participation rates?
- Do energy savings performance risk reduction products lead to lower consumer defaults and delinquencies on financial products or higher participation rates?

**Rationale B: Some consumer market segments are under-served by private capital markets**

Many consumers have adequate access to attractive capital today to overcome efficiency's high first cost barrier.[14] However, others do not (e.g., small businesses, affordable multifamily property owners and tenants) (Bell et al. 2013). In many cases, private financial markets do not serve these consumers well or serve them only with relatively unattractive, high cost products because the perception is that lending to certain market segments represents too high a risk relative to the potential financial return. It may be that information, through the collection of performance data, will be sufficient to make financing more accessible to these consumers (see Rationale C below).

However, there are some market segments that may be deemed by private lenders as unprofitable to serve, regardless of better performance data. Even if EE financing outperforms relative to other types of financing, this outperformance may not be sufficiently large to fundamentally alter the costs and risks required to deliver capital to these more difficult-to-serve consumers.

While private monies typically seek purely financial return, tax payer and utility bill payer funds target a range of system and public benefits (e.g., cost effective energy savings, reduction of environmental impacts of electricity production, diversification of resource mix to reduce various risks). This more holistic view may lead to a different assessment of risk and return based on broader programmatic goals, and may warrant long-term provision of tax payer or bill payer direct loan capital, or credit enhancement to private markets, to deliver attractive capital to overcome barriers to adoption for hard to reach market segments.[15]

Key questions:
- What market segments are currently underserved by capital markets and why?
- Which market segments are likely to continue to be underserved even if the problems underlying other rationales are addressed?
- Can attractive capital be extended to underserved consumers at "acceptable" risk to those consumers and in a way that delivers low-cost energy savings to tax payers and utility bill payers?

---

[14] For example, most owners of Class A commercial space and most public entities are deemed creditworthy by private markets and have access to a range of private financing tools (see, for example, Borgeson & Zimring 2013).
[15] It is important to note that this more holistic risk assessment and delivery of capital must be done ca3refully as the consequences of customer financing defaults can be severe and have unintended consequences.

**Rationale C: More information is needed for private financing markets (e.g., lenders, investors) to take over**

A range of financial tools and capital providers already exist to enable consumers to borrow funds to pay for the up-front cost of energy efficiency improvements. However, the terms (e.g., interest rate, loan length) and underwriting criteria of these products may not reflect all of the potential benefits that financed improvements deliver to consumers. For example, energy savings from these investments reduce consumer utility bills – in some cases by more (over the life of the improvements) than the cost of the energy improvements themselves. This financial benefit, in theory, should reduce consumer defaults on financial products relative to financing for other types of activities (e.g., boat purchase, granite kitchen countertops) because it leaves consumers with more money with which to repay their debt.[16] Lower consumer defaults should yield some combination of reduced interest rates, longer loan lengths, and less restrictive underwriting criteria (so that more consumers qualify for financing). Lower interest rates and longer loan lengths would enhance project cash flows by reducing a consumer's regular interest and principal payments and might support broader consumer EE adoption and deeper per-project energy savings.

Today, however, financial institutions lack access to adequate data to assess and price both energy savings and the improvement in borrower financing repayment trends that these savings may deliver. EE financing programs have often been limited in scale, data recording methods have not been standardized and, since many programs were launched as part of ARRA, have not existed long enough to capture default rates over a full loan cycle (Hayes et al. 2011). This information asymmetry may lead to credit rationing (Palmer et al 2012), where private markets do not deliver an adequate supply of attractive capital to this market. Financial products whose terms and underwriting are based solely on consumer characteristics or the value of collateral (and not the potential energy saving benefits of the financed projects), may be relatively unattractive compared to those that would be offered if more information were available to financial institutions. These less attractive financial products may, in turn, inhibit consumer adoption of energy efficiency.

In this context, tax payer and utility bill payer-supported financing programs could be used as temporary interventions to deliver more attractive and accessible financial products than are available in private markets today, while developing the requisite data on both project energy savings and the impact of that energy savings on financing product performance. This data could be used to substantiate to financial institutions the benefits of offering financing for efficiency improvements and enable a transition to fully-private financing markets in the future that account for these attributes. It is important to note that EE financing programs have been operating for several decades and have not so far been structured or documented in a way that has led private capital providers to alter their risk assessments of this market (and, in some cases, program volumes have not been large enough to warrant their attention).

Key questions:
- Does financing for energy efficiency have lower consumer defaults and delinquencies than financing for other property improvements? If so, what is the cause of these differences (e.g., is it specific

---

[16] Lower defaults may also be associated with unique features of EE adopters that are not captured in typical creditworthiness analysis, but may increase their predisposition to repay financing.

product characteristics, characteristics of early adopters, the presence of energy savings, or something else)?
- Is the performance of EE financing strong enough to warrant substantial improvements to the interest rates, loan lengths and/or underwriting for private financial products? Items unaffected by credit risk such as marketing, underwriting and back office processing often account for a substantial portion of financial product costs. If material financial product improvements are warranted, for which consumer segments or EE improvement types?
- What data are required to enable financial institutions to obtain sufficient evidence to improve the terms of their current product offerings? How long will it take to build this data set?[17,18]

Rationale D: Financial product standardization and aggregation are needed for private markets to deliver attractive capital

EE financial products, particularly those in the residential and small business sectors, tend to be quite small in terms of loan size. Financial institutions often participate profitably in markets like this by offering consumers standardized products that can be originated in high volume,[19] aggregated and re-sold to other investors through a highly-organized secondary markets transaction (which re-capitalizes financial institutions with sufficient monies to originate more loans or leases).[20] Today, however, the EE-specific financing market is characterized by low volume, lack of product standardization,[21] and the absence of vehicles to aggregate financing pools for re-sale.[22]

Tax payer and utility bill payer-supported financing programs could be used as a temporary or long-term intervention to standardize financial product terms across financial institution partners and/or to aggregate these financial products and facilitate secondary markets transactions. This access to secondary markets has the potential to deliver large pools of institutional investor capital for energy efficiency financing.

---

[17] The U.S. Department of Energy is currently supporting a loan data scoping study to develop best practices EE financing data collection and analysis protocols. Preliminary results will be available in 2014.

[18] Some financial institutions have been motivated to participate in energy efficiency financing pilots primarily for the reputational benefits or for opportunities to cross-sell efficiency customers into other financial products rather than the direct financial returns available from EE financing (Zimring 2011).

[19] Standardization entails consistent financial product origination and servicing protocols, so that a loan or lease originated in California is similar to a loan or lease originated in Oklahoma or New York. This standardization is essential to the process of successfully aggregating and selling these financial products in sufficient volume to attract large pools of low-cost investor capital.

[20] The re-sale of financing products is known as a "secondary" sale as the primary sale is the financial institution's origination of the financial product for the borrower. Financial institutions typically earn fees when they sell financial products to secondary investors.

[21] In the residential sector, many state & local governments used ARRA monies to launch financing programs with local financial institution partners (e.g., credit unions, community banks). Governments typically offered credit enhancements to financial institutions in exchange for interest rate, loan term or underwriting concessions. While many innovative agreements were structured, this innovation came at the cost of standardization. As some programs and their financial institution partners exhaust the money they have available to lend, they have faced challenges in selling their loan pools to "secondary markets" investors due to investor liquidity concerns and lack of historical data to use for loan pool performance modeling.

[22] The Warehouse for Energy Efficiency Loans (WHEEL) model, which relies on a subordinated capital credit enhancement from program administrators, is designed to pool standardized, unsecured residential EE loans for sale to secondary investors.

Key questions:
- What are the real barriers to the development of secondary markets for EE financing? A few efficiency programs have faced capital constraints due to high financing volume,[23] but most programs and their financial partners have substantial outstanding lending capacity.
- Will "self-organized" secondary markets pathways emerge without programmatic intervention if adequate consumer financing demand and product volume develops?
- Does sufficient consumer demand exist today to warrant program investments in aggregation and securitization infrastructure, or should interventions simply focus on increasing the volume of standardized loans?

**Rationale E: Larger consumer cost contributions are needed to increase the leverage of limited tax payer or utility bill payer funding**

The focus on financing by some policymakers and program administrators is driven primarily by a desire to encourage substantial cost contributions by participating consumers in order to stretch the impacts of limited tax payer and utility bill payer funding in the face of aggressive energy savings goals. Other financial incentives (e.g., rebates and tax credits) can also be effective in reducing efficiency's first cost hurdle and have proven their efficacy in driving consumer EE adoption. However, rebates deliver limited leverage and financing programs may increase this leverage.[24,25] For example, programs offering financial institutions a 10 percent loan loss reserve have the potential to leverage each $1 of tax payer or bill payer funds into a total of $10 of investment in EE improvements (see Table 2).[26]

**Table 2.** Sample leverage potential of EE program funds allocated to rebates compared to credit enhancements.

| Program Incentive | Potential Leverage of Program Funds[27] |
|---|---|
| 25% Rebate | 4:1 (for every $1 rebate, $4 total is invested in EE) |
| 50% Rebate | 2:1 |
| 5% LLR | 20:1 |
| 10% LLR | 10:1 |

Generally speaking, however, the private market for financing property improvements is large, sophisticated and mature. "High first costs" may be an important barrier in some situations, but is there actually a market failure in delivering adequate pools of attractive capital through existing financial

---

[23] Several EE financing programs have recently completed or are pursuing a secondary markets transaction (e.g., Pennsylvania's Keystone HELP program, New York's Green Jobs-Green New York program and Oregon's Clean Energy Works Oregon on-bill program).
[24] Residential home performance energy efficiency programs often offer rebates of 25 to 50 percent, yielding between two and four dollars of total EE investment for each rebate dollar expended.
[25] While rebates may deliver limited short-term leverage, utilized as part of market transformation strategies to build customer demand and reduce product costs, these tools may deliver very large long-term leverage.
[26] Many American Recovery and Reinvestment Act (ARRA)-funded EE financing programs targeted residential EE improvements and utilized five to 10 percent loan loss reserves (LLRs). LLRs are a form of credit enhancement that sets aside a limited pool of funds from which lenders or investors can recover a portion of their losses in the event of borrower defaults.
[27] Table 1 provides several examples of program designs that offer program funds/incentives to leverage customer investment in efficiency, ignoring program administration costs.

products that would provide the rationale for using tax payer and utility bill payer funds? Financing programs can only deliver on their leverage potential to the extent that they drive (or enable) consumer demand for EE. For many consumers and consumer classes, lack of **demand** for EE – not access to attractive capital to pay for these upgrades – may be the primary challenge. If program administrators reduce support for other program strategies in favor of financing, and consumer demand does not materialize, they risk missing their energy savings targets or other goals. Financing can (and often should) be combined with other strategies (labeling, rebates, contractor training, etc.), but the right mix of strategies is something that needs to be carefully considered and tested. Ultimately, the "consumer demand" issue is central to any strategy's potential to reach EE policy goals.

Key questions:

- Is financing an effective tool for driving consumer EE adoption? For which consumers and at what cost?
- What other strategies should be combined with financing to maximally increase demand at the lowest possible cost?

The rationales described in this chapter highlight the thought process and key questions that policymakers and program administrators should consider before launching new financing programs or committing to increasing their reliance on existing financing initiatives. It is also important to compare the realized cost and effectiveness of financing programs compared to other options for intervening in efficiency markets; we explore questions relevant to this level of inquiry in Chapter 3.

## Chapter 3: Is Financing the Best (or only) Option?

Once rationale(s) for supporting an EE financing program are identified and evaluated, it is important to assess the overall effectiveness of financing in driving consumer adoption of EE relative to – or in addition to – other possible strategies.

The up-front cost of efficiency investments is just one of many barriers, and often times not the most important one.[28] A range of non-financing program strategies and other activities (e.g., rebates, technical assistance, labeling, codes & standards, workforce training, etc.) target other barriers to efficiency adoption such as lack of consumer understanding of EE benefits, uncertainty about energy improvement performance, or an inadequate supply of qualified EE service providers. As shown in Figure 3, financing is part of a holistic suite of strategies targeting multiple barriers to consumer EE adoption.

> 2. Does financing address key barriers better or at a lower cost than other options for intervention?
>
> (i.e. Is financing the best option for solving this problem?)

It is important to recognize that developing and supporting EE financing program infrastructure can have substantial costs.[29] Thus, as a practical matter, program administrators (and policymakers) must often weigh and decide whether the decision to offer financial products will lead to budget reductions for other program strategies or elements, particularly if they are operating in a zero sum program budget environment.[30] Therefore, it is important that program administrators assess whether financing interventions can achieve program goals (e.g., scale, cost-effective energy savings, equitable consumer access to programs) as, or more, effectively – and at lower tax payer or utility bill payer cost – than these other strategies, and for which consumer segments.

---

[28]For example, some individuals and businesses are debt averse or would rather spend available capital on more compelling investments. Some businesses and institutions that have limited or no staff capacity or have already invested in relatively short payback efficiency measures and remaining opportunities have payback times that exceed their preferred internal rates of return on investments. In many cases, the societal benefits (e.g., including environmental externalities) and benefits to utility systems of energy efficiency projects exceed the short-term private benefits to consumers. (Borgeson et al. 2012)

[29]For example, the California Public Utilities Commission (CPUC) has budgeted $8M for utility information technology upgrades to accommodate On-Bill Repayment pilots and $9M of administration and implementation costs as part $75M of EE financing pilots to be operated from 2013-2015 (CPUC 2013).

[30]In a few cases, program administrators are testing whether simply marketing existing market-rate financial products will drive or enable consumer EE adoption at low program cost. There is little data today on the potential efficacy of this lower-cost strategy in driving cost-effective energy savings.

**Figure 3:** Strategies to drive and enable consumer demand for EE (SEE Action 2013).

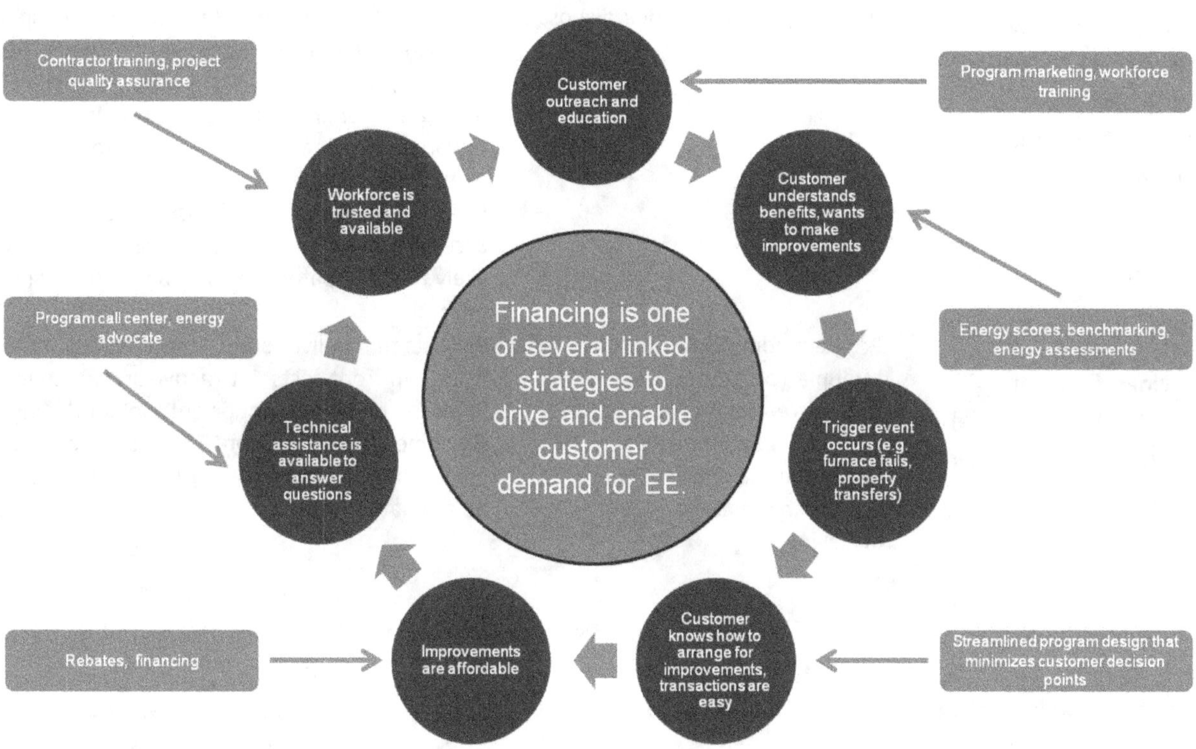

[Diagram: Central circle states "Financing is one of several linked strategies to drive and enable customer demand for EE." Surrounding circles (clockwise from top): Customer outreach and education; Customer understands benefits, wants to make improvements; Trigger event occurs (e.g. furnace fails, property transfers); Customer knows how to arrange for improvements, transactions are easy; Improvements are affordable; Technical assistance is available to answer questions; Workforce is trusted and available. External boxes with arrows: Contractor training, project quality assurance; Program marketing, workforce training; Energy scores, benchmarking, energy assessments; Streamlined program design that minimizes customer decision points; Rebates, financing; Program call center, energy advocate.]

In Table 3, we highlight several examples of financing program design questions and discuss their implications for the efficacy of financing relative to other program strategies in delivering energy efficiency. For illustrative purposes, Table 3 poses several either/or questions about the relative effectiveness of financing compared to rebates. We acknowledge that other strategies need not necessarily be abandoned in favor of financing and that a combination of strategies (e.g., rebates, financing) may be effective in driving consumer EE adoption while reducing overall tax payer or bill payer cost for these energy savings. A key challenge is developing the combinations of program strategies that can most effectively deliver low-cost energy savings in various customer market segments.

**Table 3:** Key questions on the relative efficacy of financing in driving and enabling consumer adoption of energy efficiency.

| Question | Issue | Discussion |
|---|---|---|
| **Are consumers as (or more) likely to adopt targeted EE improvements if offered financing rather than rebates (or other support such as technical assistance)?** | There is little evidence today that financing is as effective (or more effective) in overcoming the fundamental barrier to EE (i.e., driving consumer demand) or that it can do so at lower cost than other program strategies (Borgeson et al. 2012). | From a consumer's perspective, rebates improve the economics of projects and have been demonstrated to drive EE adoption; financing, even with no interest, simply delays payment. From a program administrator's perspective, financing, if it leads to adequate EE adoption rates, *may* reduce program costs (and rate impacts) compared to rebate programs. |

| What impact does program-sponsored financing (rather than rebates or other incentives) have on the likelihood of consumers that *already* have access to capital to adopt targeted EE improvements? | Many households and businesses already have attractive private financing options at their disposal. | Does the availability of EE-specific financing drive these consumers to adopt energy efficiency? Relatively few participants utilize program-sponsored financing when they are required to choose between financing and rebates (Nadel 1990, Stern et al 1985). If program administrators shift away from rebates towards financing, what impact will this have on overall market penetration and participation rates? For those households and businesses that do *not* have access to attractive financing tools, will they be more likely to participate in EE programs if financing is offered? |
|---|---|---|
| Do projects deliver greater energy savings if program financing is used (or available) compared to rebates (or other strategies)? | Program administrators have multiple goals that often include both increasing the number of consumers adopting EE and increasing the depth of energy savings that each consumer is achieving. | Projects that deliver deep energy savings often have higher up-front costs. Attractive and accessible financing *may* be an important tool for driving those consumers that do adopt EE to make more comprehensive improvements; this hypothesis should be evaluated. |

Assessing the relative value of financing compared to other interventions is not a simple activity; we discuss some methods for evaluating this important issue in Chapter 5. In most cases, program administrators will need to go beyond asking participants whether they "needed" financing to do a project or whether they "want" financing in addition to rebates or other support. It is easy to get the answers we want to these questions without necessarily obtaining an indication of the true efficacy of program-sponsored financing. Instead, program administrators will need to *test* different program offerings and observe who participates, who does not, and at what cost.

We also acknowledge that "temporal variability" (e.g., the value of supporting EE financing initiatives and the mix of financing products and programs one might choose to offer) may vary through time depending on evolving market conditions. For example, program-sponsored financing tools that rely on novel security (e.g., PACE, OBF) may be more effective during periods of weak real estate markets when households and businesses lack access to property-secured financing vehicles (e.g., mortgages, home equity lines of credit) that have traditionally supported much U.S. household and business borrowing for property improvements. Similarly, financing programs may be more effective during periods when private sector interest rates are high; thus, low-cost programmatic financial products are relatively more attractive compared to a market environment of low private market interest rates.

## Chapter 4: What Financing Program Features Best Drive Demand?

In addition to setting clear rationales for operating an EE financing program and evaluating whether financing is the most effective means for reaching program targets, new and existing financing programs can also benefit from better understanding which specific program design attributes are *most* effective in driving or enabling EE adoption– and for which consumers.

This chapter identifies a number of key program design features (e.g., financial product interest rate, term, repayment mechanism, ease of use) and poses questions for administrators to consider about the extent to which these specific design features can **drive consumer adoption** of targeted efficiency improvements. These questions, along with some discussion on each, are included in Table 4.

3. What specific financing program design features best drive demand for energy efficiency?
(i.e. How do you design the financing program for greatest impact?)

Any feature that might affect consumer EE demand is important, but examining those that are most costly to program administrators to offer is a good place to start. It is important to know whether incentives such as interest rate buy downs or credit enhancements (e.g., loan loss reserves) actually have a significant positive impact in driving EE adoption. Other financing program elements are "free", but enabling their use requires expending political capital to pass legislation or change policy rules through regulatory proceedings (e.g., OBF, PACE); thus, it is important to better understand the impacts of these features on consumer demand.

**Table 4:** Key questions exploring financing program design features.

| Question | Issue | Discussion |
|---|---|---|
| **Do lower interest rates, longer financial product maturities and/or less restrictive underwriting than what is available in private markets *increase* consumer adoption of targeted EE improvements? How important is timely and streamlined loan approval to increasing consumer adoption?** | These features may help drive consumer adoption of EE. However we lack basic information about consumer elasticity of demand around interest rates and loan terms,[31] and little data has been collected about how relaxed (or alternative) underwriting criteria influence consumer likelihood of investing in EE. For some consumers and contractors, fast-close, easy-to-use financial products that can be closed | Substantial program administrator and policymaker attention and resources have focused on improving financial product access and terms (see Rationale C from Chapter 2). Better understanding of which product features are most important in increasing EE adoption—and for whom— would help to better target resources such as credit enhancements. |

---

[31] While substantial resources are often targeted to interest rate reductions, the difference in monthly consumer payment on a 10-year, $10,000 loan with 7% vs. 10% interest loan is relatively small (~$16/month), and has uncertain impacts on consumer EE adoption.

| | | |
|---|---|---|
| | at the consumer's "kitchen table" may be more effective in driving EE adoption than low-interest/long-term financial products with higher transaction costs (e.g., closing at the bank). | |
| **Is offering EE financing to consumers that lack access to capital in private markets more or less effective in catalyzing consumer adoption of targeted EE improvements than for other consumers?** | Offering EE financing to consumers that lack access to other sources of capital to pay for these improvements may be more effective in driving consumer EE adoption than it is for the broader consumer base. | Consumers that lack access to sources of capital may be "debt averse" and more concerned about the consequences if energy savings do not materialize and they are unable to make debt service payments compared to other consumers. Significant resources are often allocated to expanding consumer access to capital, but, in many cases, the average program participant would qualify for existing private financial products. Better understanding of the non-financing barriers to EE adoption amongst consumers that lack access to attractive private financial products may enable limited program resources to be allocated more effectively. |
| **Does the ability/willingness to repay EE financing on a tax or utility bill increase consumer adoption of EE improvements relative to traditional financial products?** | The consumer convenience of repaying financing on an existing tax or utility bill may reduce consumer debt aversion, facilitate the contractor sales process, or otherwise increase the uptake of EE improvements relative to offering financial products that are repaid on a separate bill. These benefits may be particularly effective with on-utility bill repayment, where a single bill might show the energy savings for which a consumer is making debt service payments and those payments. | Uncertainty remains about whether the primary value of novel financial products is their unique security features (which may improve product terms or expand access to capital) or their capacity to help drive consumer adoption of EE because they offer a more convenient repayment mechanism. Certain product features (e.g., primary residential PACE lien, on-bill tariff structure) may be politically or legally difficult to implement, and a better understanding of the value of these tools in increase consumer EE adoption would help policymakers understand the importance of various product features. |
| **Does expected (or realized) "bill neutrality" increase consumer adoption of targeted EE improvements?** | Expected bill neutrality (i.e.,– the expectation that consumer energy savings will be at least as large as consumer financing payments) may be a compelling tool for driving consumer adoption of EE, but its efficacy remains largely untested. Energy savings is often a sales "hook," but many consumers decide to move forward with energy improvements to solve other household or business problems (e.g., comfort, aging or failed equipment) (Fuller et al 2010). Realized energy savings also tend to vary from expectations and the consequences for market development of consumers not realizing the expected level | Requiring bill neutrality may restrict the depth of an energy savings project can achieve. Given uncertainty about their impacts on both driving consumer EE adoption and/or enhancing repayment trends, caution is warranted as this feature may "lock" programs out of delivering some of the deep energy improvements that may be necessary to achieve broad energy saving policy goals. |

| | of energy savings are uncertain. | |
|---|---|---|
| **Do energy performance guarantees increase consumer adoption of targeted EE improvements?** | Energy performance guarantees that ensure a consumer will receive a specified level of energy savings (or insurance that covers energy savings underperformance) may be compelling tools for driving consumer adoption of EE, but their efficacy remains largely untested in most market sectors (with the exception of public/institutional markets where ESCOs have been relatively successful). | It is estimated that Energy Service Companies (ESCos), which offer Energy Savings Performance Contracts (ESPCs) that guarantee consumers will achieve expected energy savings, have penetrated approximately 30 percent of local, state and federal EE markets and over 40 percent of K-12 schools (Larsen et al. 2013). ESCOs have had more limited success in offering ESPCs in other market sectors. |
| **Is offering multiple financing products (or having multiple financial institutions offering the same product) more effective in driving consumer adoption of targeted EE improvements than offering a single financial product (or having a single financial institution partner)?** | Some EE financing programs offer multiple financing products (or have multiple financial institutions offering similar products and competing for consumer business). Others offer a single financial product (or have a single financial partner). A single option might simplify the contractor sales process and avoid financing becoming an additional complex decision that consumers must make. However, some consumers may value the option to pick the financial product that best suits their needs from a suite of multiple program-supported product offerings. Having multiple products or partners may also encourage competition and innovation. | It remains unclear whether single or multiple options are more effective in driving consumer adoption of EE improvements. Reducing uncertainty about which approach is most effective, and for which consumers, would have substantial impact on program design as many administrators are pursuing "open market" models through which any qualified financial institution may compete to deliver EE financing products to consumers and/or contractors. |
| **Does automatic or optional transferability of financing payments increase consumer adoption of targeted EE improvements?** | Transferability is the automatic or optional transfer of the obligation to pay a financing charge from one tenant to the next or from one property owner to the next. This feature may increase consumer willingness to invest in EE improvements with paybacks that exceed their expected tenancy in, or ownership of, a building because they may be positioned to transfer the remaining charge to the subsequent building occupant when they move. | If subsequent tenants & owners do not value the EE improvements, they may not accept the charge or may reduce the price they are willing to pay to purchase or occupy a property. This leads to uncertainty about whether transferability will increase consumer EE adoption. Substantial policymaker resources are often allocated to implementing transferable financial products despite the lack of evidence that consumers adopt EE or adopt deeper EE improvements when this feature is present. |

In the next chapter we discuss some of the methods and resources for evaluating these questions.

# Chapter 5. Evaluating Key Questions

Policymakers and program administrators in a number of states are interested in relying more heavily on EE financing, often as part of a strategy to increase the leverage of limited ratepayer or public monies. While financing programs are promising for some consumers, these initiatives have not been subjected to rigorous evaluation techniques. Before administrators make more substantial commitments to financing – particularly if those commitments require reducing investments in other program strategies – it is important that policymakers and administrators clearly define the specific problems their financing programs are designed to overcome and integrate evaluation techniques that can reduce the uncertainty about whether these initiatives are effective tools for driving consumer adoption EE at low long-term cost. Chapters 2 to 4 describe many of the key questions which must be explored to reduce the uncertainty about financing's effectiveness in delivering on policy maker and program administrator goals.

There are a range of techniques and levels of effort that can be applied to answering these questions. Some questions are best analyzed through qualitative approaches such as market research, discussion with program staff and stakeholders, and informal observation over time. However, to address other questions, more robust and quantitative approaches are necessary. These evaluation efforts require upfront planning, take time to assess, and may involve a significant $$ investment in program evaluation. In some cases they involve collecting and analyzing potentially sensitive consumer data or involve implementing controlled experiments. But, they are often the only way for us to know whether our interventions are working and can better enable policymakers and program administrators to make informed choices about how to allocate limited tax payer and utility bill payer resources.

In this chapter, we describe three broad categories of evaluation activities that program administrators and policymakers can consider. Evaluation categories are discussed in order of confidence that policymakers and administrators can have in drawing definitive conclusions from such activities:[32]

1. Qualitative market research (lower confidence);
2. Analysis of standardized financing program data; and
3. Experimental design and quasi-experimental design (higher confidence).

## 1. Qualitative Market Research

In some cases, policymakers and program administrators will have to make judgment calls on appropriate programmatic approaches using a range of qualitative techniques (e.g., research on experiences from other emerging financial markets, interviews with program participants and potential financial partners, and focus groups). Qualitative market research can be an effective way to understand how potential market participants and consumers think about EE financing and their perspectives on the importance of various program elements. The text box below provides an example of a key question—the need for programs to support the development of secondary markets—for which qualitative research might be the best approach to resolving uncertainty.

---

[32] These techniques are not, in many cases, mutually exclusive.

*Example:* Secondary Markets Development

In Chapter 2, we asked whether self-organized secondary markets might emerge in the absence of programmatic interventions if sufficient EE financing volume existed. In several states (e.g., New York, Pennsylvania), program administrators are utilizing public or quasi-public entities to aggregate EE financial products and ultimately facilitate their sale to secondary investors. Initial sales of these project loan pools to secondary buyers has required the provision of credit enhancements, which, depending on loan default rates may have substantial costs to program administrators. Whether these interventions are the best use of public or utility ratepayer resources is a question worthy of qualitative consideration by policymakers and administrators, but not one that lends itself well to rigorous testing. In cases with limited direct experience and significant uncertainty, one approach is to look to the past experiences of other emerging financial markets (e.g., time shares) for evidence on how EE finance markets might evolve and to make strategic decisions based on these other markets. Another approach is to implement "no regrets" actions, such as product and program standardization across jurisdictions, which are necessary precursors to the development of robust secondary markets, in order to buy time for private markets to respond on their own without the risk of over-committing programmatic resources to strategies that might ultimately prove unnecessary or ineffective. After a period of time, policymakers and program administrators could then revisit the question with additional data and experience in hand.

## 2. Analysis of Standardized Financing Program Data

The standardization of financing program data collection and analysis is an important approach to resolving several foundational questions regarding the performance of financing for efficiency projects. This approach is best suited to answering broad questions whose answers are unlikely to vary dramatically across small differences in specific program design elements or financial product features. In the text box below, we describe how standardizing the collection of EE project and loan data can be used to better understand the performance of EE financing. There is currently active research and inquiry by the U.S. Department of Energy and the State of California into what financing data can and should be collected to enable better analysis of EE financing programs. The standardization of data collection may have co-benefits, such as informing efforts to reflect the value of EE improvements in property values.

*Example:* EE Financing Default Rates

In Chapter 2, we noted that, at present, some/many financial institutions have claimed that they lack access to adequate data on actual vs. estimated energy savings from efficiency projects and the improvement in borrower financing repayment trends that these savings may deliver. Collecting and analyzing data from the increasing number of EE financing programs operating in local and regional markets may be able to reduce this information gap. However, no single program is large enough (in volume or geographic coverage) to deliver the large data sets across geographies that are necessary for financial markets to assess whether consumers default or become delinquent at lower rates for EE financing than for other financial products. The diversity of program sponsors and lack of clear protocols for collecting and sharing data across programs makes assembling this EE financing performance data challenging.

Standardizing data collection and analysis protocols across these financing programs is a powerful tool for aggregating sufficiently large pools of data to bridge this information gap. This standardization will ensure that the performance data from pools of EE financing in New York is relatively similar to that from pools of EE financing in California – and that this data is broadly available for analysis. In the event that analysis of data from these financing programs does not demonstrate conclusively that efficiency financing programs out-perform other financial products to warrant better product terms from financial markets, then program sponsors may need to use experimental design techniques to assess what specific financing program, project and consumer attributes are most likely to deliver on EE financing's promise of low default rates (see next section).

## 3. Experimental and Quasi-experimental Design

Across the country, most EE programs deliver a range of services (e.g., rebates, financing, technical assistance, contractor training) that may impact the consumer's propensity to invest in – or repay financing for – EE improvements. The higher the number of factors that may influence target consumer behaviors (e.g., EE adoption, financing repayment), the more difficult it is to identify the impacts of *specific* program design features on the desired program outcome.

Qualitative assessments are unlikely to yield answers to many of the program design questions described in this report with sufficient confidence that it would be prudent for administrators and policymakers to rely solely on them in designing a finance program or making substantial shifts in resource allocations towards financing. Similarly, standardizing data collection and analysis is unlikely to yield answers to research questions related to the efficacy of specific program design elements or financial product features in driving consumer EE adoption. Instead, experimental and quasi-experimental design techniques are the best techniques for answering the detailed questions identified in Chapters 3 and 4 about whether EE financing can drive consumer adoption of cost-effective EE at lowest public or ratepayer cost, and what specific financing program features are most effective in achieving administrator goals. As policymakers and administrators increasingly seek to assess the cost-effectiveness of EE financing programs, resolving these foundational questions is essential.

Experimental and quasi-experimental design approaches hold as many program delivery factors as possible constant in order to isolate and study the impact of specific financing program features. Both experimental and quasi-experimental designs typically create two groups of consumers, one of which is given the treatment[33] (the treatment group) and another which is not (the control group). The key

---

[33] The treatment is the intervention that the program is providing to program participants. For example, if a program administrator wants to test whether more customers adopt deep energy improvements if 15 year financing is offered rather than the existing 10 year product, the treatment group would be offered 15 year financing and the control group would be offered 10 year financing.

difference between the two approaches is the method used to assign participants to the treatment and control groups. **Experimental design, or a randomized control trial (RCT), uses random assignment** of participants to the two groups while **quasi-experimental design uses non-random assignment** of participants to the two groups.[34] Where program administrators expect one program design or financial product feature to be significantly more effective than another (i.e., a large effect size), quasi-experimental design may be preferable because it often avoids some of the implementation challenges that a RCT poses for administrators (e.g., market confusion, equity concerns across consumers or administrative hassle).

However, there is substantial uncertainty about the answers to many of the questions raised in this report, and program administrators should consider experimental design (i.e., RCT) both because it can detect smaller effect sizes and because it delivers the highest level of confidence that the results of the experiment are representative of the efficacy of the program design element in question at larger scale. In the text box below we provide an example of how experimental design can be used to explore the impact of bill neutrality on consumer demand. We also provide an introduction to experimental design in this section and more detailed information in Appendix A (Experimental Design Methods & Practical Experimental Design Implementation Guidance).

*Example:* Bill Neutrality

Bill neutrality (i.e., requiring that a project's expected energy savings exceed principal and interest repayment costs) may be an important driver of both consumer adoption of energy efficiency and strong financial product performance (i.e., low default rates). However, bill neutrality can restrict administrators' abilities to achieve their energy savings targets by limiting the depth of energy savings that consumers can pursue, and it may prevent consumers from investing in energy efficiency improvements that offer other perceived benefits (e.g., comfort, aesthetics, health and safety). In addition, expected bill neutrality's impact on financial product performance is uncertain given variance in realized savings from expectations and other consumer credit considerations that may play a larger role in influencing financing repayment trends (e.g., job status). Experimental design is a powerful tool for resolving uncertainty about how bill neutrality both impacts consumer adoption of energy efficiency and consumer repayment of energy efficiency financing. Consumers could be randomly assigned to two groups, one of which is offered a package of improvements that is expected to be bill neutral and another of which is not. With random consumer assignment, any difference in outcome between the two groups can be attributed to relative efficacy of the two offers.[35] While answering the question about financial product performance will take several years, program administrators will learn about whether expected bill neutrality is an important driver of consumer EE adoption.

---

[34] Where random assignment is not possible or practical, quasi-experimental design techniques assign participants to the two groups in a way that is as close to random assignment as possible. For example, if Town A and Town B share similar demographics, the town lines may form the basis of assigning households or businesses to the treatment or control group.

[35] Random assignment ensures that the customers receiving Program Offer A and Program Offer B are identical *in expectation*. After the randomization has occurred, there will likely be differences that exist between the two groups due to random chance. However, these differences are usually small and statistically insignificant.

## Introduction to Experimental Design

The goal of experimentation is to see how well specific program designs work relative to other program designs. Good experimental design creates a way to test which program or program element more effectively delivers on policy maker and program administrator goals. Experimental design is often called A/B testing: comparing the outcomes from Offer A to Offer B (e.g., a financing program vs. a rebate program, a financing program with a loan interest rate of 10% vs. 5%, etc).

### Experimental Design Basics

In an ideal hypothetical world, we would offer consumers one type of program or incentive and observe their response, and then go back in time and observe how those same consumers would respond to a different type of program or incentive (this other program type or incentive is often called the *counterfactual*). Comparing the outcomes from the two different programs offerings would tell you which program or incentive design is more effective. Unfortunately, we cannot observe this counterfactual.[36] This leaves us to use experimental design to compare two different (but similar) groups of consumers: one group of consumers given Offer A, and another group given Offer B. If the consumers are sufficiently similar, the difference in outcomes between the groups is a good estimate of the offers' relative efficacy.

### The Selection Bias Problem

Why is experimental design necessary at all -- for example, could a program administrator assess the efficacy of the two offers by just giving everyone the choice of rebates or financing and see which delivers more projects or deeper per-project energy savings?

In most cases, the answer is a *no*, due to *selection bias;* the risk that consumers that choose Offer A may have fundamental differences from consumers that choose Offer B.[37] For example, the type of households that opt for rebates (Offer A) rather than financing (Offer B) may be fundamentally different than the type of households that are more likely to choose Offer B – let's say they tend to be more interested in getting deeper energy savings. If this is the case, we might assume that rebates result in more energy saving investments than financing, even though this is not the case – it is simply that those households would have made more energy saving investments regardless of the program offer. Without experimental design, comparing the outcomes between self-selecting groups delivers results that are biased and that are unlikely to reflect the efficacy of Offers A versus B. That is, the differences in the perceived effectiveness of the two offers could be largely due to differences in the participating consumers, not the offers themselves.

### Using Experimental Design to Overcome Selection Bias

There are various experimental and quasi-experimental designs that attempt to deal with selection bias (see Table 4). All of these designs are fundamentally targeted at creating two groups of similar consumers to compare to each other. Experimental design eliminates the selection bias issue completely by randomly creating two similar groups (leading to high confidence in the validity of the results); quasi-experimental design uses non-random group selection techniques that will typically lead to results with lower confidence in their validity.[38]

---

[36] For example, if a customer is offered a financing program, and we observe that the customer installs a measure, we cannot then offer the customer a rebate for the same measure in order to compare it to financing.

[37] The exception to this answer is when administrators expect the difference in effectiveness from one offer to another to be extremely high.

[38] For a more detailed description of different types of experimental designs and the analysis needed to evaluate the designs, see: State and Local Energy Efficiency Action Network. 2012. *Evaluation, Measurement, and Verification (EM&V) of Residential Behavior-Based Energy Efficiency Programs: Issues and Recommendations*. http://behavioranalytics.lbl.gov.

**Table 5:** Design techniques for selecting control and treatment groups.

| Design | Type of design | Confidence[39] | Description |
|---|---|---|---|
| Random Assignment of Consumers (Randomized Control Trial - RCT)[40] | Experimental | **High confidence** in evaluation of any key question | Consumers are randomly assigned to receive Offer A or B. Neither the contractor nor consumer is aware of which offer the consumer will receive before developing a potential work scope. This method will deliver the highest degree of confidence that the results of one's experiment are valid. |
| Random Assignment of Contractors | Experimental | **High confidence** in evaluation of any key question | Contractors are randomly assigned to deliver Offer A or Offer B to their consumers. This method will also deliver a high degree of confidence that the results of one's experiment are valid, but requires a large number of contractors. |
| Cutoff Point[41] | Quasi-Experimental | **Relatively high confidence** in evaluation of any key question | Consumers are assigned to receive Offer A if they are above a pre-determined cutoff point or Offer B if they are below a pre-determined cutoff point. The cutoff can be any continuous variable common to all potential participants (e.g., whether the second letter of their last name is before or after M). |
| Geographic Location[42] | Quasi-Experimental | **Relatively low confidence** in evaluation; confidence depends on similarities in geographic locations | Consumers in one geographic location are given Offer A, and those in another geographic location are given Offer B. The more similar the locations (e.g., demographics, climate, etc), the higher confidence the results. |
| Time Differences | Quasi-Experimental | **Low confidence** for evaluation of many key questions | Before a certain pre-determined date, consumers are given Offer A, and after the date they are given Offer B. |

A range of considerations will impact which, if any, of these methods is most appropriate:

- **Desired level of confidence in validity of results:** Some methods allow evaluators to have a high degree of confidence that the evaluation is valid; other methods are only valid for specific types of research questions. The level of confidence depends on how similar the treatment and control groups are to each other. With an RCT, the treatment and control groups are exactly the same (in expectation), while for the Geographic Location method, the control and treatment groups are from different locations and may be very different.
- **Ease of implementation:** Some methods may fit in easily with a standard program implementation method, while others may require a very specific implementation method. RCTs require specific, randomly assigned consumers to receive different type of program offers; these consumers must be tracked. In contrast, the Time Differences method simply requires consumers to receive one type of offer before a certain date, and another type after.

---

[39] For illustrative purposes, we qualitatively assess the relative confidence on can have in these five techniques. While RCT always yields the highest confidence results, depending on the specifics of one's experiment, other techniques may also yield high confidence results. For example if the cutoff point selected is something completely arbitrary, it is likely to result in groups that are as good as randomly assigned. Similarly, if there is a geographic border that runs through a city where there are similar households on both sides of the border, then a geographic location method may yield similar confidence to a cutoff point. The exception is time differences, which is likely to yield lowest confidence results in most cases (See Appendix A for detailed explanation).

[40] Depending on the exact form of the randomization, this may also be called "recruit and delay" or "randomized encouragement design".

[41] This is also called regression discontinuity (RD).

[42] This may be called "difference-in-differences" if data on the outcome being measured is known before the offers are made.

- **Ease of data analysis:** Random assignment methods are transparent and straightforward to analyze; other methods require more difficult analyses in order to attempt to correct for inherent differences between the control and treatment groups. For example, with a Geographic design, the analysis must control for demographic and energy use characteristics of the control and treatment groups; Time Differences requires controlling for all external factors that may have occurred. The Cutoff Point requires a regression discontinuity analysis.
- **Number of consumers required:** Each research question and experimental design requires a specific number of consumers ("sample size") in order to get results that are statistically significant. [43]

Choosing an appropriate technique for selecting the control and treatment groups is one of seven steps to integrating experimental design into EE financing programs (see Appendix A for more detailed discussion on experimental design).

---

[43] The number of customers needed should be calculated by doing a statistical *power calculation*, and depends on several factors: the research question; the metric used to compare the programs; the experimental design; the minimum difference in program outcomes that would be valuable to learn (e.g., do you need to know if A is 1% better than B, or only if it's 10% better than B?); the percentage of customers that typically decide to do a retrofit after getting any kind of offer from a contractor; the variation in how much money customers spend on retrofits; and other factors.

## Chapter 6. Conclusions

It is important for administrators to challenge and verify their assumptions before making fundamental shifts in their program offerings and then consistently evaluate whether financing, and what financing program designs, are most effective in moving consumers to action in implementing energy efficiency upgrades through time. This report offers a starting place for developing a better understanding of financing's role in driving cost-effective energy efficiency adoption. We encourage program administrators and policymakers to identify those issues and questions that are most relevant to their program's success and to begin to test whether their assumptions are correct. Not every program needs to answer every question – as more and more programs actively explore these questions, lessons learned can be shared. The answers to some key questions may not vary dramatically between programs, and administrators should consider coordinating their financing evaluation efforts regionally or nationally (through new or existing forums) to take advantage of likely economies of scale. However the answers to some of these questions may differ across – and sometimes within – both consumer classes and geographies. Thus, the conclusions from program evaluation should not be overly generalized.

# References

Bell, C., Sienkowski, S. and S. Kwatra. 2013. "Financing for Multi-Tenant Building Efficiency: Why This Market is Underserved and What Can Be Done to Reach It". American Council for an Energy-Efficient Economy (ACEEE). LINK

Borgeson, M., Zimring, M. and C. Goldman. 2012. "The Limits of Financing for Energy Efficiency." Lawrence Berkeley National Laboratory. LINK

Borgeson, M. and M. Zimring. 2013. "Financing Energy Upgrades for K-12 School Districts". Lawrence Berkeley National Laboratory. LBNL-6133E. LINK

Cadmus Group. 2012. "California 2010-2012 On-Bill Financing Process Evaluation and Market Assessment." Prepared for California Public Utilities Commission. LINK

California Public Utilities Commission (CPUC). 2013. "Decision Implementing 2013-2014 Energy Efficiency Financing Pilot Programs." Decision 13-09-044 Issued 9/19/2013.

Connecticut Clean Energy Finance and Investment Authority (CEFIA). 2013. "Comprehensive Plan: FY 2013 through FY 2015." LINK

California Public Utilities Commission (CPUC). 2013. "Proposed Decision Implementing 2013-2014 Energy Efficiency Financing Pilot Programs." LINK

Cuomo, M. 2013. "NY Rising. 2013 State of the State." LINK

Eto, J. and W. Golove. 1996. "Market Barriers to Energy Efficiency: A Critical Reappraisal of the Rationale for Public Policies to Promote Energy Efficiency. Lawrence Berkeley National Laboratory. LBNL-38059 LINK

Fuller, M. 2009. "Enabling Investments in Energy Efficiency: A study of energy efficiency programs that reduce first-cost barriers in the residential sector." Prepared for California Institute for Energy and Environment and Efficiency Vermont. LINK

Fuller, M., C. Kunkel, M. Zimring, I. Hoffman, K. Soroye and C. Goldman. "Driving Demand for Home Energy Improvements." Lawrence Berkeley National Laboartory LBNL-3960E. LINK

Hayes, S. S. Nadel, C. Granda and K. Hottel. 2011. "What Have We Learned from Energy Efficiency Financing Programs?" American Council for an Energy Efficient Economy (ACEEE). LINK

International Energy Agency. 2008. "Promoting Energy Efficiency Investments: Case studies in the residential sector." ISBN 978-92-64-04214-8. LINK

Jaffe, A. and R. Stavins. 1994. "The Energy Efficiency Gap: What does it mean?" Energy Policy 22 (10): 804-810. LINK

Nadel, S. 1990. "Lessons Learned: A Review of Utility Experience with Conservation and Loan Management Programs for Commercial and Industrial Consumers." American Council for an Energy Efficient Economy (ACEEE). LINK

Palmer, K., Walls, M. and T. Gerarden. "Borrowing to Save Energy: An Assessment of Energy-Efficiency Financing Programs." Resources for the Future. LINK

State and Local Energy Efficiency Action Network Financing Solutions Working Group (SEE Action). 2013. "Using Financing to Scale up Energy Efficiency: Work Plan Recommendations for the SEE Action Financing Solutions Working Group." Prepared by Lawrence Berkeley National Laboratory and Harcourt Brown and Carey. LINK

Stern, Paul C., Elliot Aronson, John M. Darley, Daniel H. Hill, Eric Hirst, Willett Kempton and Thomas J. Wilbanks, "The Effectiveness of Incentives for Residential Energy Conservation," Evaluation Review (April 1985, Volume 10, Number 2).

Stuart, E., P. Larsen, C. Goldman and D. Gilligan. 2013. "Current Size and Remaining Market Potential of the U.S. Energy Service Company Industry." Lawrence Berkeley National Laboratory. LBNL-6300E, Harcourt Brown & Carey, Inc. (HB&C) 2011. "Energy Efficiency Financing in California Needs and Gaps. Preliminary Assessment and Recommendations." Presented to The California Public Utilities Commission, Energy Division. LINK

Zimring, M. 2011. "Austin's Home Performance with Energy Star Program: Making a Compelling Offer to a Financial Institution Partner." Clean Energy program Policy Brief. Lawrence Berkeley National Laboratory. LINK

# Appendix A. Experimental Design Methods & Practical Implementation Guidance

Appendix A describes the five experimental design methods outlined in Chapter 5 in greater detail and provides a seven step guide for integrating experimental design into EE financing programs.

The experimental design methods differ in their techniques for assigning consumers to the control or treatment groups (see Table A-1).

Table A-1: Design techniques for selecting control and treatment groups.

| Design | Type of design | Confidence[44] | Description |
|---|---|---|---|
| Random Assignment of Consumers (Randomized Control Trial - RCT) | Experimental | **High confidence** in evaluation of any key question | Consumers are randomly assigned to receive Offer A or B. Neither the contractor nor consumer is aware of which offer the consumer will receive before developing a potential work scope. This method will deliver the highest degree of confidence that the results of one's experiment are valid. |
| Random Assignment of Contractors | Experimental | **High confidence** in evaluation of any key question | Contractors are randomly assigned to deliver Offer A or Offer B to all of their consumers. This method will also deliver a high degree of confidence that the results of one's experiment are valid, but requires a large number of contractors. |
| Cutoff Point | Quasi-Experimental | **Relatively high confidence** in evaluation of any key question | Consumers are assigned to receive Offer A if they are above a pre-determined cutoff point, or Offer B if they are below a pre-determined cutoff point. The cutoff can be any continuous variable common to all potential participants (e.g., whether the second letter of their last name is before or after M). |
| Geographic Location | Quasi-Experimental | **Relatively low confidence** in evaluation; confidence depends on similarities in geographic locations | Consumers in one geographic location are given Offer A and those in another geographic location are given Offer B. The more similar the locations (e.g., demographics, climate, etc), the higher confidence in the results. |
| Time Differences | Quasi-Experimental | **Low confidence** for evaluation of many key questions | Before a certain pre-determined date, consumers are given Offer A and after the date they are given Offer B. |

## Random Assignment of Consumers

The gold standard of experimental design, and the most rigorous way to limit selection bias, is to *randomly assign* consumers to receive either Offer A or Offer B. With random consumer assignment, any

---

[44] For illustrative purposes, we qualitatively assess the relative confidence of these five techniques based on what we believe would be a typical implementation approach. While RCT always yields the highest confidence results, depending on the specifics of one's experiment, other techniques may also yield high confidence results. For example if the cutoff point selected is something completely arbitrary, it is likely to result in groups that are as good as randomly assigned. Similarly, if there is a geographic border that runs through a city where there are similar households on both sides of the border, then a geographic location method may yield similar confidence to a cutoff point. The exception is time differences, which is likely to yield lowest confidence results in most cases (see below for a more detailed explanation; basically, because homeowners are likely to invest in energy efficiency measures only once every few years (or longer), an early choice to invest in Option A is likely to preclude a later choice to invest under Option B (even if the homeowner would rather have invested with Option B), and it is therefore harder to compare Offer A to Offer B).

difference in outcome between the two groups can be attributed to relative efficacy of the two offers.[45] For this type of experimental design, consumers are randomly assigned to receive one of two offers, A or B (e.g. rebates or financing; 5% or 7% interest rate loans).

Choosing when to conduct randomization and when to present the program offer to a customer is a function of the question being tested and ease of implementation for any given program. For example, a program administrator may wish to test how a consumer responds to different types of offers that a contractor makes (e.g., what causes consumers to complete more upgrades: an offer of financing or rebates). In this case, the key aspects of the experimental design are:

- Consumers are randomly assigned to receive either Offer A or Offer B;
- Consumers are not initially aware of which offer they will receive; they learn this only during the contractor's "pitch"; and
- Contractors do not choose which households to approach based on which group they are in and therefore which offer they will receive.[46]

One common technique for implementing random assignment is to set up an easy-to-access system that allows contractors to determine whether a consumer should receive Offer A or Offer B at the time the contractor is making the offer (e.g., contractors could call a 1-800 number, use an iPhone app). The consumers could be pre-randomized at the start of the experiment, with these assignments maintained in a database, and only made available to a contractor once a consumer has been engaged. Alternatively, consumers could be randomized at the moment the contractor is about to make the pitch and recorded in a database at that time.

If an administrator wants to test what offer motivates consumers to show more interest in energy efficiency (i.e., is advertising rebates or financing more likely to cause consumers to call a contractor to setup an energy assessment?), the administrator would pre-randomize consumers and then target the control or treatment group offer to consumers up-front, perhaps through a mailed advertisement.

### *Potential Challenges*

The analysis method used to assess the efficacy of the two offers is relatively straightforward and transparent and involves comparing the average results of the group that received Offer A to the group that got Offer B.[47] The main drawback to this method is that it may be practically difficult to implement as contractors may be reluctant to add uncertainty to their sales process. Consumers may also hear (and complain) that other consumers were offered a different deal. Program administrators may want to consider testing Offers whose net economics are similar (e.g. $1,000 rebate v. $1,000 interest rate buy

---

[45] Random assignment ensures that the customers receiving Offer A and Offer B are identical *in expectation*; after the randomization has occurred, there will likely be differences that exist between the two groups due to random chance. However, these differences are usually small and statistically insignificant.

[46] If the contractor knows which customers will receive Program Offer A or B before contacting customers, the contractor may introduce bias by only pursuing leads with customers receiving one offer or the other. The contractor might also present recommendations to the customer in different ways; in which case the results would reflect the preferences of the contractor, not the choices of the customer.

[47] Other evaluation methods require complicated analyses that rely on collecting detailed information on consumers to control for as many consumer differences as possible and isolate the impact of the program element being studied.

down) to reduce concerns about fairness. In cases where program administrators are concerned that consumers or contractors will be unwilling to accept randomization, using a Cutoff Point design is often the second best approach.

## Cutoff point

A good alternative to randomized assignment is assigning consumers to the control or treatment group based on a **cutoff point** – consumers above the cutoff point get Offer A and consumers below the cutoff point get Offer B. This works because consumers very close to the cutoff on either side are likely to be similar to one another. The cutoff point can be based on anything that takes on a continuous range of values and that the contractor is not aware of before they approach a consumer. The best cutoff points are those that are likely to have very little relationship to consumer characteristics that might be connected to the research question (e.g., is the third letter of the consumer's name before or after the letter "M" rather than does the consumer earn more or less than $50,000) because it increases the likelihood that consumers far from the cutoff point will resemble those that are closer to it. This method relies primarily on comparing the outcomes of those consumers close to the cutoff point on either side.[48] While we can have a high degree of confidence about the results from this method for the consumers close to the cutoff point, in order to extend the results to all consumers, we must assume that consumers that are far away from the cutoff point will react similarly to those near the cutoff point.

### Potential Challenges

This type of experimental design is a very good alternative when randomization is not feasible. It will ensure a relatively high degree of confidence that the results are valid and is easier to implement. It is important that contractors are unaware of which side of the cutoff the consumer is on before beginning the energy efficiency sales process. If contractors are aware of which side each household is on, they might only sell to those consumers that have been selected to receive Offer A, biasing the results. Ideally, contractors would ask consumers for information at the point of sale that would allow them to determine which program offer to make.

## Geographic location

A third experimental design choice is assigning consumers to Offer A or Offer B based on geographic location (e.g., consumers in one neighborhood in a utility territory versus consumers in another similar neighborhood in a utility territory). Results from this experimental design are only valid insofar as one believes that the consumers in the different locations are similar. For example, if the geographic dividing line is in the middle of a street, so that one group is across the street from the other, consumers may be very similar. However if the geographic dividing line is state or county lines, those lines may be drawn in places with distinctly different demographics (e.g., dividing urban and rural locations, or wealthy and poor communities). The consumers in two different counties may be very different and the results from comparing the two groups to each other may therefore not be valid. Another issue is that there is no way to hide consumer locations from the contractors. Contractors will therefore be aware of which consumers

---

[48] Customers closest to the cutoff are the most comparable, while those further away from the cutoff are less comparable. An analysis method called regression discontinuity is the best way to analyze experimental designs based on a cutoff point; it puts more weight on those closest to the cutoff.

will receive which Offer ahead of time, which risks biasing the results because differences in outcomes could be driven by contractors not consumers.

*Potential Challenges*

This type of experimental design may be acceptable if two locations with similar consumers can be found and could be preferable compared to not doing a pilot program that is evaluated. Because there is little that can feasibly be controlled in this design, implementation is relatively easy. The type of analysis for this design should attempt to control for every observable consumer trait (e.g., income, historical energy use, current energy use, home sale price, age, number of occupants, etc.) that may vary across geographic locations, and is therefore somewhat difficult.

## Time differences

A fourth choice is assigning consumers to Offer A or B based on time differences. Those that apply before a certain date are assigned to Offer B and those that apply after that date are assigned to Offer A. This type of design should only be used in the case that Offer A is known with certainty to be better than Offer B, but program administrators are seeking to better understand the magnitude of the difference on consumer EE adoption patterns. For example: Offer A is 5% financing, Offer B is 10% financing; 10% is offered before a certain date, and 5% is offered after that date. Consumers must be unaware that the offer will switch from Offer A to Offer B on a certain date. If possible, the date that the offer switches from A to B should be during a time that a change in outcomes is most attributable to the change in programs. For example, if most building retrofits occur during the summer, then the date should be in the middle of the summer so that changes in consumer activity can be observed apart from seasonal changes in demand.

*Potential Challenges*

This type of experimental design will only produce results that are meaningful for one very specific type of research question: if A is known to be better than B, and B is offered first and A is offered second. It will produce invalid results if the research question is whether A or B is better, or if A is known to be better and A is offered first. Even for the specific research questions for which this test is appropriate, the experimental design is still somewhat problematic and there is likely to be uncertainty about the validity of the experiment's results. This type of analysis attempts to control for every observable consumer trait (e.g., income, historical energy use, current energy use, home sale price, age, number of occupants, etc.), and every observable event that changed over time (e.g., employment rates, interest rates, etc.) and is therefore challenging.

This design has several issues. If consumers are aware that there is going to be a different program available after a certain date, consumers may postpone or accelerate energy upgrades to correspond with the program offer that they prefer. This phenomenon could lead to a large selection bias because the consumer groups would not comparable. Even if consumers are unaware that the program will change from B to A at a certain date, assigning consumers based on a cutoff date is challenging because some energy improvements may be investments that consumers make infrequently – perhaps every 10 or 15 years or longer. This is not a decision that a consumer makes every day or month.[49] Moreover, in practice, it may not be easy to offer the "better" program second; consumers who decided to get retrofits with the first offer may be unhappy once they realize that a better program is now offered (e.g., lower financing interest rates).

## Randomize at Contractor Level

Another option is to randomly assign contractors to different programs, rather than assigning consumers to different programs. For example, contractors randomly assigned to group A are allowed to offer consumers rebates, while contractors in group B are allowed to offer consumers financing. This type of design answers slightly different questions than the previous designs. Rather than answering whether providing *consumers* with Offer A or Offer B is better, it answers whether giving *contractors* the ability to sell Offer A or Offer B is better. Because this design randomizes contractors, there will be a high degree of confidence in the validity of results.

### *Potential Challenges*

The main issue with this type of design is that because the randomization is done at the contractor level rather than the consumer level, there must be many more participating contractors than in other designs.[50] Randomly assigning contractors is relatively easy to implement, if a large enough group of contractors can be found. Because it is randomized, the results will be valid and robust. The analysis must account for the fact that consumers targeted by one contractor may be different than consumers targeted by another contractor and so it is a slightly more difficult analysis than a design that randomizes at the consumer level.

---

[49] To see why this is a problem, consider three cases. In the first case, suppose that one is trying to test which program, A or B, is better. Also suppose that 10 customers would choose to do a retrofit with program A, 15 would choose to do a retrofit with program B, and 25 would decide to do a retrofit with either A or B. If A is offered first and B second, then 35 customers would get retrofits with A, and 15 would get retrofits with program B. One might conclude that A is much better than B, even though in fact program B is better at getting people to do retrofits. If B is first and A second, 40 would get retrofits with B, and 10 with A; one might conclude that B results in 30 more retrofits than A, when in fact it only results in 5 more. In the second case, suppose that A is known to be better than B (e.g., A is 5% financing, and B is 10% financing), and one is trying to test how much better A is. Also suppose that while 50 customers would choose to get retrofits with program A, only 20 would get retrofits with B. If A is offered first and B is offered second, then all 50 customers would get retrofits with program A, and then 0 would get retrofits with program B. One might conclude that A results in 50 more retrofits, when in fact 20 of those people would have chosen retrofits under program B, and so A only results in 30 more retrofits. If A is known to be better than B, and B is offered first and A second, then in our example 20 customers would choose retrofits under program B, and then when the better program A is offered second, 30 additional customers would choose retrofits. Then the additional 30 retrofits could accurately be attributed to program A. In addition, there are other factors that change over time that may affect the way customers react (e.g., changes in the economy, new customers entering the market, changes in interest rates, changes in social culture, etc.).

[50] The number of contractors that would need to be included should be determined using a statistical power calculation; the sample size required may be as much as 100 times that required by randomization of customers. This power calculation will also take intra-class correlation into account and will depend on how many customers each contractor accesses as well as the variance of customers both within and across contractors.

## Practical Experimental Design Implementation Guidance

This section offers a seven step guide for integrating experimental design into EE financing programs (see Figure A-1).[51]

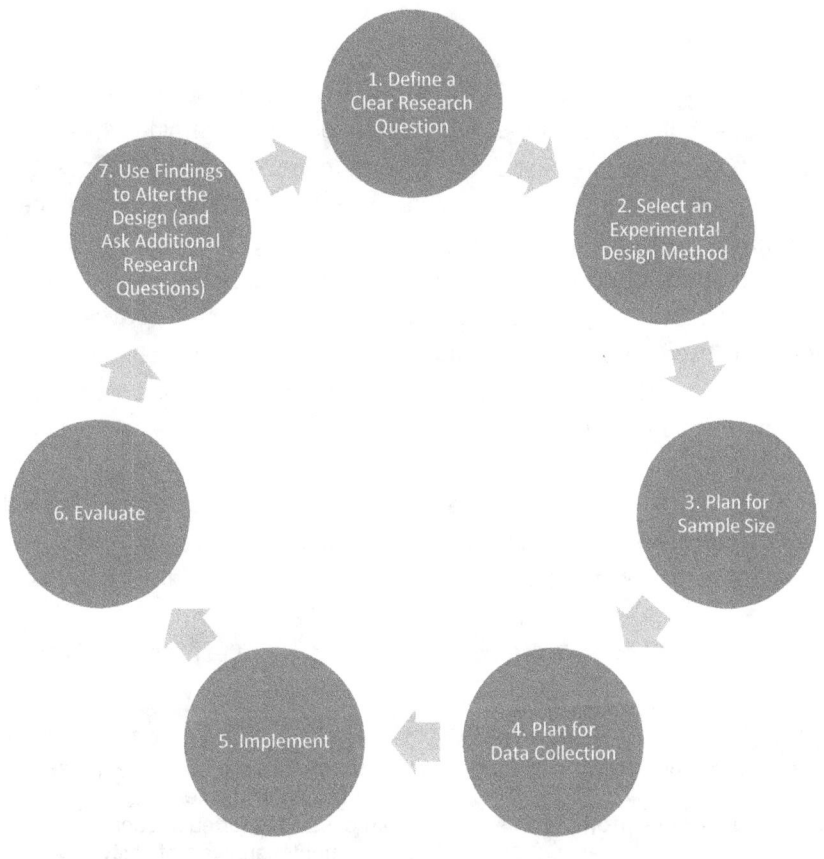

**Figure A-1:** Overview of seven steps for effectively integrating experimental design into EE financing programs.

### 1. Define a Clear Research Question

The first step in integrating experimental design into an energy efficiency financing program is deciding on a specific research question to test. It is important to make sure that the research question is clear and precise. There are three keys to developing a strong research question:
- Define what you are comparing;
- Define the outcome to be measured; and
- Define the consumers that you are targeting.

---

[51] There are many qualified consultants and evaluators that can help set up these designs. This is intended as a primer to familiarize policymakers with the benefits of experimental design and the importance of doing experimental design right.

*What are you comparing?*

Energy efficiency programs do not exist in a vacuum; their effectiveness is always relative to other types of initiatives or no initiative at all. For example, a new financing program could be compared to a rebate program, compared to no program (i.e. no financing or rebates), or compared to the status quo program (e.g., on-bill financing v. unsecured off-bill loans).

- **Weak Research Question**: "Is on-bill financing effective?"
- **Strong Research Question**: "Does the availability of on-bill financing increase consumer EE adoption rates in the single family residential sector relative to the availability of unsecured financing?"

*What outcome will you measure to determine which program offer is more effective?*

It is important to be clear about what outcomes will be measured to determine which program offer is more effective. For example, you might care about the performance of a pool of unsecured loans versus a pool of on-bill financing loans. In this case, the outcome that you would want to measure is default rates or number of late payments. Another outcome might be which program results in more contractor conversions of consumer leads to consumer projects. You might also want to measure the types of projects that are being completed through each offer and the level of energy savings they are achieving.

- **Weak Research Question**: "Is on-bill financing effective relative to off-bill unsecured financing?"
- **Strong Research Question**: "Does the availability of on-bill financing result in higher per-project energy savings relative to standard financing in the single-family residential sector?"

Explicitly stating the outcome of interest will help to make clear what data needs to be collected. Data accessibility should, therefore, be an important consideration when defining the outcome measure. Table A-2 includes examples of outcome variables that may be of interest to program administrators.

**Table A-2:** Sample outcomes to be measured in evaluating the effectiveness of financing programs.

| Outcome Measure | Data Collection Needed |
|---|---|
| Which offer results in more consumers adopting EE improvements?** | Whether or not each consumer presented with an offer adopted EE improvements |
| Which offer results in deeper per-project EE savings?** | Depth of savings for each consumer that adopted EE improvements; analysis of utility bills |
| Which offer results in specific targeted types of retrofits (e.g., "deep" retrofits vs. lower cost retrofits with fewer measures) | Whether or not each consumer completed specific types of home upgrade (e.g., whether each consumer chose to perform weather-stripping, wall insulation, window replacements, etc.) |
| Which offer results in lower-default rates on financial products? | Whether or not each consumer defaulted on loan payments over the life of the financial product |
| Which offer results in more cost effective, energy savings? | Per-project program expenditure relative to per-project energy savings |

** This data should be collected for any research question

*Which consumer classes are you targeting?*

The answers to many of the questions raised in this report are likely to vary across (and sometimes within) consumer classes. It is important to appropriately target experiments to ensure that the results are not overly generalized.

For example:

- The way in which a large institutional consumer responds to a five versus seven percent interest loan is likely to differ markedly from the way in which a single-family homeowner responds to these interest rate differences.
- Middle income households may be more motivated to pursue energy upgrades (or invest in deeper upgrades) by a program financing offer than a rebate incentive relative to their higher income peers (who may be more likely to have ready access to attractive capital).
- "Bill neutrality" expectations or guarantees may increase a high energy use household's willingness to take on financing for deep energy saving projects compared to these features' impacts on low energy users.

Defining which consumer classes you are targeting is an important part of a strong research question.
- **Weak Research Question**: "Does on-bill financing result in more consumer spending on energy efficient products relative to standard financing?"
- **Strong Research Question**: "Does on-bill financing result in more spending by single family residential consumers on energy efficient products relative to standard financing? Does this differ for high income households relative to middle & low income households?"

Table A-3 includes examples of different consumer market segments within the single family residential sector; similar breakdowns could be done for multifamily and non-residential consumers.

**Table A-3:** Examples of single family residential consumer market segment.

| Consumer Grouping | Data Collection Needed |
|---|---|
| High income vs. low income consumers | The income band that each consumer belongs to (e.g., less that 50k, 50-75k, etc.) or the census block of each consumer that can be linked to geographic income data from the U.S. Census[52] |
| Elderly vs. young consumers | The age band for every consumer (e.g., less that 18, 18-25, 25-35, etc.), or the census block of each consumer that can be linked to age data for the head of household from the U.S. Census |
| Owners vs. renters | Whether each consumer is a property renter or owner or the census block of each consumer that can be linked to ownership data from the U.S. Census |
| High vs. low floor area | The square footage of each home |
| Other residential consumer characteristics | Data for each consumer on characteristics of interest that might play a role in their program participation, or U.S. Census block data for each consumer on:<br>✓ Employment status<br>✓ Educational status<br>✓ Number of occupants<br>✓ Value of home<br>✓ Existing heating or cooling system |

---

[52] Census block data is useful if there is a household characteristic that is available in census data that: (a) you believe corresponds to large differences in outcomes, and (b) that the characteristic varies widely across the census blocks that you are studying but does not vary widely within each census block. Household-level survey data is more useful if the characteristic that you would like to test varies widely within census blocks, or you expect small differences in outcomes between the characteristic groups you are testing. For example, it would be useful in the case that you believe that income strongly affects a household's decision to adopt financing over rebates, and that the income of most households within a census block are relatively close to the average income of the census block. Then you could draw conclusions, such as that households in high income neighborhoods tend to choose financing over rebates 20% more often than households in low income neighborhoods.

## 2. Select an Experimental Design

The goal of experimental design is to answer the research question that you have developed. There are several tradeoffs to consider when deciding on the appropriate experimental design: which design produces results that are more robust and valid, which design is easiest to implement, which design requires the easiest analysis, and which design requires a smaller number of consumers.

## 3. Plan for Sample Size

Each research question and experimental design requires a specific number of consumers ("sample size") in order to obtain results that are statistically significant. It is essential that the sample size is planned in advance;[53] if there are too few consumers, then effort may be wasted on designing and implementing an experiment because too little data will be collected to complete an analysis. The easiest way to ensure that there will be enough consumers is to structure the pilot so that it operates for an open-ended amount of time until that sample size has been reached.

## 4. Plan for Data Collection

In addition to obtaining a sufficient sample size, the appropriate data must be collected in order to answer each research question. It is critical that program implementers develop and vet a data collection plan up-front to ensure that their experimental design efforts will yield results.

If the research question is stated in a clear and precise way, the data needed to answer the question should be evident. For **any research question**, two pieces of data are necessary at a minimum:
(1) whether the consumer received Offer A or Offer B; and
(2) whether or not the consumer accepted the offer.

Depending on the **outcome measure** defined in the research question, additional data will be needed (see Table A-2 for examples of data needed for specific outcome measures). Depending on the **target consumer classes** defined in the research question, additional consumer characteristic information may be needed (see Table A-3 for examples of relevant consumer information that may need to be collected). It is very important that all necessary data is collected for every consumer that is offered Offer A or Offer B, *even if* they don't accept the offer, and even if they don't decide to do any energy improvements.

There are various ways to collect the necessary data; often data may be available through existing program processes and protocols. Contractors, utilities or financial institutions are often responsible for ensuring that accurate data is submitted in a timely fashion. Program administrators should consider whether a small financial incentive is appropriate to encourage contractors (or other third parties) to provide this data (and to compensate them for the added time it might take to submit it).

---

[53] The number of customers needed depends on several factors and is calculated by doing a statistical power calculation The research question, the metric used to compare the programs, the experimental design, the minimum difference in program outcomes that would be valuable to learn (e.g., do you need to know if A is 1% better than B, or only if it's 10% better than B?), the percentage of customers that typically decide to adopt a retrofit after getting any kind of offer, the variation in how much money customers spend on retrofits and a range of other factors can all impact this calculations.

## 5. Implement

Consumers should be assigned to a control or treatment group and care should be taken to ensure that consumers receive the appropriate program offer. It is useful to keep track of all steps and procedures that are followed during the experiment to refer to during the evaluation.

## 6. Evaluate

Depending on the type of experimental design selected, different types of analyses are required. An experienced evaluator will be able to offer advice on the type of analysis required for the specific design and the level of experience and technical competence required.

## 7. Use Findings to Alter Program Design (or Setup New Experiment)

If properly designed, evaluations can provide administrators with useful information on the role of financing (or specific financial product features). Administrators can use these results to alter program design or to setup additional experiments to hone in on program offers that will be most effective in driving different consumers to efficiency at lowest ratepayer or public cost.

www.ingramcontent.com/pod-product-compliance
Lightning Source LLC
Chambersburg PA
CBHW081803170526
45167CB00008B/3308